★ ★ ★ ★ ★ ★ ★ ★ ★ ★ ★

THE
BILL OF RIGHTS
AND
RESPONSIBILITIES

★ ★ ★ ★ ★ ★

A Book of Common Sense

★ ★ ★ ★ ★ ★

★ ★ ★ ★ ★ ★ ★ ★ ★ ★ ★

THE
BILL OF RIGHTS
AND
RESPONSIBILITIES

★ ★ ★ ★ ★ ★

A Book of Common Sense

★ ★ ★ ★ ★ ★

By Stephen Smoke

GENERAL PUBLISHING GROUP
Los Angeles

Publisher: W. Quay Hays
Editor: Peter Hoffman
Art Director: Gaston Moraga
Projects Manager: Trudihope Schlomowitz
Production Director: Nadeen Torio

Library of Congress Cataloging-in-Publication Data

Smoke, Stephen.
    The Bill of Rights and responsibilities / by Stephen Smoke.
    p.   cm.
    ISBN 1-881649-86-5
    1. Human rights. 2. Responsibility. I. Title.
    JC571.S656   1996
    323—dc20   96-15775
                                          CIP

Printed in the USA
10 9 8 7 6 5 4 3 2 1

General Publishing Group
Los Angeles

Dedication

To my late Grandmother, May Wise.
As a working widow, she raised five children during the Depression, without public assistance, teaching by example the values contained in self-reliance and personal
responsibility. Despite working for wages
that, even when converted to 1996 dol-
lars, most high school dropouts today
would consider well beneath their dignity,
my grandmother always managed to have
something left over at the end of the day
for others less fortunate who always knew
to come to her back door for small
amounts of food, and much larger help-
ings of respect and human kindness.

Introduction

If we want to understand rights and responsibilities, we must first understand that, with very rare exceptions, all rights have underlying explicit or implicit responsibilities attached to them. This is as true of governments and the people they govern as it is of businesses and their customers, husbands and wives, parents and children, students and teachers.

Therefore, it is important to know what our responsibilities are as they pertain to the many relationships in our lives. What responsibilities, spoken or unspoken, legal and/or moral, do we have to our spouses? To our children? Our parents? Our neighbors? Our employers? Our employees? Our customers?

Several generations of Americans have grown up with a very sketchy understanding of the rights granted to them by the Constitution. Most people haven't the vaguest notion that those rights are tied to any responsibilities. You often hear people scream, "I know my rights!," but when was the last time you heard someone yell, "I know my responsibilities!"?

More than any particular right or responsibility, the entire concept of rights and responsibilities has been lost in an often well-intentioned campaign to ensure that everyone knows his or her rights and that no one ever, under any circumstances, has those rights violated.

Today, there is a perception that rights are free, that they come with the birth certificate and require no responsibility on the part of those receiving such rights. It is as if people believe that those rights have always existed and always will. But they haven't always existed—200 years is but the blink of an eye in the history of man—and it is unclear whether those rights will be preserved as we know them, or in any form, in the future.

The frightening thing about this lack of understanding that rights are inextricably linked to responsibilities is that many people truly believe they can have rights without responsibilities. And while you can have rights without responsibilities for a time, history as well as common sense tells us that rights without responsibilities ultimately leads to chaos and, often, violence, both in personal relationships and in society at large.

With generations of people unfamiliar with personal responsibility—a concept sometimes literally scoffed at in a culture that reveres and rewards the victim—the notion that people should shoulder responsibility is often considered punitive and, in fact, an infringement upon their rights.

It is curious that young people will often say, "This is America. I have the right to do whatever I want to do." Clearly, this is a tremendous misunderstanding of America and the concept of rights in general. There are many things people can't do. American citizens have more freedom than citizens of any other country in the world, but that freedom is explicitly limited by state and federal laws, and implicitly limited by what remains of social mores.

Rights and responsibilities are linked whether we wish them to be or not. A society that grants rights without responsibilities will become an irresponsible society whose citizens can say and do anything, regardless of potential harm to others, without fear of consequence. Such a society encourages the press to be more outrageous than accurate. It encourages an obsession with what feels good to "me," without considering the effects of the individual's actions on others—because "I have the right to be happy, and I have no responsibility to anyone else." It encourages self-esteem without linking it to personal responsibility or achievement. It encourages people to resolve their conflicts via lawsuits rather than common sense.

In short, it becomes a society isolated into tiny groups whose individual interests always outweigh the good of society as a whole. It becomes a dangerous society in which people are afraid of their neighbors because they know their neighbors feel no responsibility toward them.

We are all responsible, whether we want to be or not, for what ultimately becomes of this country. A nation aware of its rights and unaware of its responsibilities is a nation headed for disaster.

At its core, this book strives to create an awareness of the intrinsic link between rights and responsibilities. In fact, this is not a new concept, it's just an idea that needs to be rediscovered. John Kennedy said, "Ask not what your country can do for you; ask what you can do for your country." No one laughed then, but that was back in an age when patriotism and personal responsibility weren't looked upon as the radical principles of some kind of right wing conservative manifesto. Some Americans have never known a time when it was "cool" to call yourself an American. To some citizens, patriotism is a joke, the flag is just a piece of cloth and responsibility is for suckers.

I firmly believe that most Americans don't believe that.

*A*merica might be better served
If we focused as much on a
Bill of Responsibilities
As we do on the Bill of Rights.

$\mathcal{M}$r. Roosevelt has contributed greatly to the end of Capitalism in our own country, although he would probably argue the point at some length. He has done this, not through the laws which he sponsored or were passed during his Presidency, but rather through the emphasis he put on rights rather than responsibilities."

John F. Kennedy

*Y*ou have the **right** to dream about your goals.

★ ★ ★ ★ ★ ★

*I*f you want to accomplish your goals, you have the **responsibility** to do the work required to make them happen.

You have the **right** to teach your children to respect themselves.

★ ★ ★ ★ ★ ★

You have the **responsibility** to teach them to respect others as well.

You have the **right** to teach your children to feel good about themselves.

★ ★ ★ ★ ★ ★

You have the **responsibility** to teach them values and behavior that will make that feeling come easily.

$\mathcal{Y}$ou have the **right** to assume that your child knows right from wrong.

★ ★ ★ ★ ★ ★

$\mathcal{Y}$ou have the **responsibility** to realize that these days nothing goes without saying.

*Y*our children have the **right** to watch TV in your home.

★ ★ ★ ★ ★ ★

*Y*ou have the **responsibility** to inform yourself about what they are watching.

*Y*our children have the **right** to learn about and explore the Internet.

★ ★ ★ ★ ★ ★

*Y*ou have the **responsibility** to set guidelines and do your best not to expose them to influences and ideas you deem inappropriate in your home.

You have the **right** to say anything you wish to say on the Internet.

★ ★ ★ ★ ★ ★

You have the **responsibility** to realize that your words and actions are the building blocks of an enormous structure in which all our children, to some degree, will one day work and play.

*Y*ou have the **right** to say that you are stunting your children's development when you don't expose them to every aspect of "real life."

★ ★ ★ ★ ★ ★

*Y*ou have the **responsibility** to recognize that you don't have to break your arm to know it's painful, or to shoot up heroin to realize it's dangerous; there is no logic that leads to the conclusion that if you experience lots of sex and violence during your formative years, your life will be better or that you will be more empowered in any way.

*Y*our child has the **right** to expect a quality education from his or her school.

★ ★ ★ ★ ★ ★

*Y*our child has the **responsibility** to recognize that his or her conduct plays a part in the educational process. (And you have the responsibility to make sure your child understands this.)

*Y*ou have the **right** to spoil your kids.

★ ★ ★ ★ ★ ★

*Y*ou have the **responsibility** to make sure they don't grow up spoiled.

You have the **right** to buy things for your kids.

★ ★ ★ ★ ★ ★

You have the **responsibility** to teach them the value of money and what is required to make it.

*Y*ou have the **right** to teach your children at home.

★ ★ ★ ★ ★ ★

*Y*ou have the **responsibility** to see that they learn not only *about* people, but how to get along with, and relate to, people as well.

You have the **right** to think it's cute when your 10-year-old daughter's idea of conflict resolution is suing one of her little friends.

★ ★ ★ ★ ★ ★

You have the **responsibility** to teach your children that litigation should *always* be the very *last* resort to problem solving.

You have the **right** to provide for your family.

★ ★ ★ ★ ★ ★

You have the **responsibility** not to steal from another family in order to do so.

*Y*ou have the **right** to gamble.

★ ★ ★ ★ ★ ★

*Y*ou have the **responsibility** to your-self and your family not to risk more than you can afford to lose.

*Y*oung adults have the **right** to live their lives free from parental interference.

★ ★ ★ ★ ★ ★

*I*f they want to be treated as adults, they have the **responsibility** to take care of themselves (and not make *their* problems—financial and otherwise—their *parents'* problems).

Children have the **right** to expect their parents to take care of them.

★ ★ ★ ★ ★ ★

Grown children have the **responsibility** to help the parents who helped them.

You have the **right** to nurture your inner child.

★ ★ ★ ★ ★ ★

You have the **responsibility** to make sure your inner child doesn't grow up to be a bloated and selfish brat.

You have the **right** to be alone.

★ ★ ★ ★ ★ ★

You have the **responsibility** to realize that life is a team sport.

You have the **right** to seek your own counsel.

* * * * * *

You have the **responsibility** to educate yourself so that your counsel will be wise.

You have the **right** to believe that money is the measure of a man.

★ ★ ★ ★ ★ ★

You have the **responsibility** to rethink your concept of human weights and measures.

You have the **right** to criticize the greedy actions of wealthy people.

★ ★ ★ ★ ★ ★

You have the **responsibility** to recognize that you don't have to be wealthy to be greedy, and that not all wealthy people are greedy.

I have the **right** to dream new dreams.

★ ★ ★ ★ ★ ★

I have the **responsibility** to follow them, and know when they are too far gone to catch.

I have the **right** to be an individual.

★ ★ ★ ★ ★ ★

I have the **responsibility** to realize that I live in this world with lots of other individuals.

*A*ccording to TV and print ads, I have the **right** to "get in your face."

★ ★ ★ ★ ★ ★

I have the **responsibility** to understand not everyone likes me being in his face just as I would not like someone in mine.

I have the **right** to vote.

★ ★ ★ ★ ★ ★

I have the **responsibility** to honestly educate myself, over and above television advertisements, about the candidates and issues I vote for.

I have the **right** to make mistakes.

★ ★ ★ ★ ★ ★

I have the **responsibility** to learn from those mistakes.

I have the **right** to be wrong.

★ ★ ★ ★ ★ ★

I have the **responsibility** to learn the difference between right and wrong.

$\mathscr{I}$ have the **right** to feel and express my good intentions.

★ ★ ★ ★ ★ ★

$\mathscr{I}$ have the **responsibility** to realize that effective actions do more good and help more people than all the good intentions in the world.

$\mathscr{I}$ have the **right** to be creative.

★ ★ ★ ★ ★ ★

$\mathscr{I}$ have the **responsibility** to understand that many people don't appreciate originality.

I have the **right** to be negative and cynical.

★ ★ ★ ★ ★ ★

I have the **responsibility** to realize the damage it eventually does to myself and those around me.

$\mathscr{I}$ have the **right** to express my opinion about someone.

★ ★ ★ ★ ★ ★

$\mathscr{I}$f what I say reflects negatively on that individual, I have the **responsibility** to make sure that what I say is accurate, and I must remember that others have the right to express their opinions about me.

$\mathscr{I}$have the **right** to expect good service
and respect from a waiter or waitress.

★ ★ ★ ★ ★ ★

$\mathscr{I}$have the **responsibility** to show
respect and good manners to the waiter
or waitress serving me, and reward
their service.

I have the **right** to thumb my nose at society.

★ ★ ★ ★ ★ ★

I have the **responsibility** to understand if society thumbs its nose at me.

*I*f you are a Democrat or if you are a Republican, you have the **right** to be offended (or not) when someone in a public forum says vicious, cruel and exaggeratedly false things about the men and women in whom you believe and put your trust.

★ ★ ★ ★ ★ ★

*Y*ou have the **responsibility** to be equally offended (or not) when someone in a public forum says vicious, cruel and exaggeratedly false things about the men and women in whom *others* believe and put their trust.

I have the **right** to raise my voice to protest what I believe to be wrong.

★ ★ ★ ★ ★ ★

I have the **responsibility** to lower my voice so that my neighbors can exercise that same right.

You have the **right** to practice your own religion.

★ ★ ★ ★ ★ ★

You have the **responsibility** to afford others the same freedom, including those who choose not to practice any.

You have the **right** believe there is no God.

★ ★ ★ ★ ★ ★

You have the **responsibility** to tolerate those who believe there is.

You have the **right** to say, "You don't understand me because I'm different than you."

★ ★ ★ ★ ★ ★

You have the **responsibility** to hear me when I say, "You don't know my heart."

You have the **right** to say you have been discriminated against.

★ ★ ★ ★ ★ ★

You have the **responsibility** to hear me if I say that I have never discriminated against you, even though others have.

*E*very American has the **right** to ride any bus, use any restroom and eat in any restaurant he wishes.

★ ★ ★ ★ ★ ★

*E*very American has the **responsibility** to remember that this was not always so for every American.

You have the **right** to say that your ancestors were slaves and that slavery was wrong.

★ ★ ★ ★ ★ ★

You have the **responsibility** to hear me when I say that I never owned a slave and that I too believe slavery was, and still is, wrong.

I have the **right** to say that I'm not prejudiced.

★ ★ ★ ★ ★ ★

I have the **responsibility** to recognize and combat prejudice in my home, in my workplace, in my community, in my country and, especially, in my own heart.

You have the **right** to be outraged when a defenseless African American is beaten by whites.

★ ★ ★ ★ ★ ★

You have the **responsibility** to be equally outraged when a defenseless white man is beaten by African Americans.

We *all* have the **responsibility** to be outraged when a defenseless person of any race or gender is beaten by ANYONE!

𝒴ou have the **right** to say that the United States is the most racist country in the world.

★ ★ ★ ★ ★ ★

𝒴ou have the **responsibility** to explain why millions of people of all races and nationalities continue to risk their lives to come to the United States.

You have the **right** to say that there are racists in America.

★ ★ ★ ★ ★ ★

You have the **responsibility** to realize that that doesn't make America a racist country. (There are Amish people in America, but that doesn't mean America is an Amish country.)

You have the **right** to say that there are anti-Semites in America.

★ ★ ★ ★ ★ ★

You have the **responsibility** to realize that that doesn't make America an anti-Semitic country.

You have the **right** to say that some blacks hate all whites in America.

★ ★ ★ ★ ★ ★

You have the **responsibility** to realize that that doesn't mean that all blacks hate whites.

You have the **right** to say I'm a racist.

★ ★ ★ ★ ★

You have the **responsibility** to prove it.

*A*s an African American you have the **right** to say that racism is the reason for your disappointments and failures.

★ ★ ★ ★ ★ ★

*W*hile that is undoubtedly true in some cases, you have the **responsibility** to realize that more blacks than ever have achieved success in the past ten years and under conditions that were the same or similar to your own.

As a woman you have the **right** to say that you have been discriminated against.

* * * * * *

While that is undoubtedly true in some cases, you have the **responsibility** to realize that more women than ever have achieved success in the past ten years and under conditions that were the same or similar to your own.

As a white male you have the **right** to say that Affirmative Action has led to discrimination against you.

★ ★ ★ ★ ★ ★

While that is undoubtedly true in some cases, you have the **responsibility** to realize that being a white male in the United States still offers you incredible opportunities.

*A*s an artist you have the **right** to say that no one understands your work.

★ ★ ★ ★ ★ ★

*A*s an artist who wishes to communicate—if in fact that is one of your goals—it is your **responsibility** to make yourself understood.

As a citizen and voter you have the **right** to say you want to cut government spending.

★ ★ ★ ★ ★ ★

You have the **responsibility** not to act so surprised and offended when some of those cuts affect you.

You have the **right** to lobby for the government to do more.

★ ★ ★ ★ ★ ★

You have the **responsibility** to realize that the government needs money to do things, and that the only money the government has comes from you.

I have a **right** to get paid for the work I do.

★ ★ ★ ★ ★ ★

I have a **responsibility** to perform my duties to the best of my abilities.

An employer has the **right** to hire a "conflict resolution" specialist who accommodates complainants and refuses to make any person wrong because it might damage the person's self-esteem.

* * * * * *

The employer also has the **responsibility** to realize that this type of conflict resolution discourages personal responsibility, is demoralizing to employees who can still tell right from wrong and encourages frivolous lawsuits.

*Y*ou have the **right** to tell an employee he has done something wrong.

★ ★ ★ ★ ★ ★

*Y*ou have the **responsibility** to tell him when you are happy with his work.

$\mathscr{A}$ company has the **right** to demand that its employees and management recognize and assume at least some personal responsibility for their actions.

★ ★ ★ ★ ★ ★

$\mathscr{A}$ company has the **responsibility** to its employees to be personally accountable for its own actions.

As an employee you have the **right** to have your grievance heard.

★ ★ ★ ★ ★ ★

You have the **responsibility** to realize that, unless you have been purposely mislead, you have at least some, though not necessarily an equal, personal responsibility in the matter.

$\mathscr{A}$s a United States citizen you have the **right** to protection under all United States laws.

★ ★ ★ ★ ★ ★

$\mathscr{Y}$ou have the **responsibility** to see that the law is preserved, respected and meted out evenly to all, regardless of race, creed, color and (politically correct) cause.

I have the **right** to the protection and privileges guaranteed to citizens of the United States by the Constitution and the Bill of Rights.

★ ★ ★ ★ ★ ★

I have the **responsibility** to obey the laws of this country and work within that system to change those laws I believe to be wrong or unfair.

You have the **right** to be outraged when a police officer beats a suspect or criminal.

★ ★ ★ ★ ★ ★

You have the **responsibility** to be out-raged when a suspect or criminal beats a police officer.

Police officers have the **right** to use force when necessary to keep the peace.

★ ★ ★ ★ ★ ★

They have the **responsibility** to know when force is necessary, and not to use it excessively.

*Y*ou have the **right** to criticize incompetent and brutal police officers.

★ ★ ★ ★ ★ ★

*Y*ou have the **responsibility** to actively support good police officers.

A lawyer has the legal **right** to financially destroy and humiliate another human being in a courtroom in order to earn his fee.

★ ★ ★ ★ ★ ★

A lawyer has the **responsibility** to be aware that there is no one more dangerous than someone who has nothing left to lose.

Lawyers have the **right** to tell their clients that right or wrong has nothing to do with the outcome of a case.

★ ★ ★ ★ ★ ★

They have the **responsibility** to change the law so that it does.

Lawyers have the **right** not to be "completely honest" in court.

★ ★ ★ ★ ★ ★

They have the **responsibility** to explain to their children the difference between not being completely honest and lying.

Lawyers have the **right** to be "purposely vague" in court.

★ ★ ★ ★ ★ ★

They have the **responsibility** to explain to their children the difference between being purposely vague and lying.

Lawyers have the **right** to practice law.

★ ★ ★ ★ ★ ★

They have the **responsibility** to recognize that an outcome based on being "not completely honest" and "purposely vague" causes people to lose faith in lawyers and the law.

Lawyers have the **right** to feel that the law is too complex for "common people."

★ ★ ★ ★ ★ ★

They have the **responsibility** to recognize that this says more about the inadequacy of the law than it does about people.

Lawyers have the **right** to argue anything.

★ ★ ★ ★ ★ ★

They have the **responsibility** to realize that just because you can come up with an argument for something doesn't mean that it is fair or just.

Lawyers have the **right** to say they work in the "justice system."

★ ★ ★ ★ ★ ★

They have the **responsibility** to admit that most of them now work in the "legal business."

Lawyers have the **right** to say that they have no choice but to try to win acquittals for clients they know to be murderers and rapists.

★ ★ ★ ★ ★ ★

Lawyers have the **responsibility** to understand why members of the community into which these criminals are then released hate them for it.

The media has the **right** to praise hooded gang members and put their photos on the front page for not killing each other during a truce.

★ ★ ★ ★ ★ ★

They have the **responsibility** to explain why kids who make tougher choices, braver choices and resist getting into gangs in favor of getting an education, are rarely deemed worthy of the front page.

I have the **right** to clean air and fresh water.

★ ★ ★ ★ ★ ★

I have the **responsibility** to involve family and friends in recycling in the home and the workplace, to support causes I believe help maintain and improve the environment and to under-stand and balance environmental con-cerns with the concerns of the people who live in that environment.

You have the **right** to walk down a public street anytime day or night.

★ ★ ★ ★ ★ ★

You have the **responsibility** to realize that some people mistakenly believe they own those streets, and to be alert.

The media has the **right** to focus on
and glorify murderers and other criminals.

★ ★ ★ ★ ★ ★

They have a **responsibility** to realize
that this encourages others to seek
that spotlight.

$\mathscr{I}$ have the **right** to write a book.

* * * *. * *

$\mathscr{I}$f I'm capitalizing on having committed a crime or on the sensational nature of the trial surrounding a crime, I have the **responsibility** to realize that such a project may further victimize the persons who have already suffered the most, and that not everyone will believe that my primary motivation is to "set the record straight."

$\mathscr{I}$ have the **right** to argue that, theoretically, nothing is inherently good or bad, right or wrong.

★ ★ ★ ★ ★ ★

$\mathscr{I}$ have the **responsibility** to realize that real life is not theoretical.

I have the **right** to equal opportunity.

★ ★ ★ ★ ★ ★

I have the **responsibility** to realize that it is my choice to either take advantage of those opportunities or not. (And I must bear in mind that a guarantee of an opportunity is not the same as a guarantee of a result.)

*Y*ou have the **right** to be offended
when someone disrespects you.

★ ★ ★ ★ ★ ★

*Y*ou have the **responsibility** to ask
yourself if you were respecting that person before they "dissed" you.

You have the **right** to say that
America should be isolationist.

★ ★ ★ ★ ★ ★

You have the **responsibility** not to get
upset when other governments don't
treat their citizens the way you think
they should.

*Y*ou have the **right** to be outraged when you learn of United States intelligence being involved in the overthrow of a foreign government.

★ ★ ★ ★ ★ ★

*Y*ou have the **responsibility** to appreciate United States intelligence when a building or plane used by you or your family was not destroyed by terrorists because of behind-the-scenes United States intervention.

*Y*ou have the **right** to call the American flag a symbol of tyranny.

★ ★ ★ ★ ★ ★

*Y*ou have the **responsibility** to realize that most people, in this country and around the world, do not share your beliefs.

You have the **right** to be disgusted when corporations abuse their workers.

★ ★ ★ ★ ★ ★

You have the **responsibility** to be equally disgusted when an employee extorts money from a corporation by making false claims and by filing lawsuits that have no merit.

You have the **right** to vote against cost-cutting measures that require personal sacrifice.

★ ★ ★ ★ ★ ★

You have the **responsibility** to create a future for your children.

You have the **right** to have sex with any other consenting adult in private.

★ ★ ★ ★ ★ ★

You have the **responsibility** to take responsibility for the results of that sexual encounter, even if the result turns out to be a pregnancy.

A woman has the **right** to choose to drink and do legal drugs while she's pregnant.

★ ★ ★ ★ ★ ★

*S*he has the **responsibility** to realize that her baby has no such choice.

You have the **right** to demonstrate against the system of government of the United States.

★ ★ ★ ★ ★ ★

You have the **responsibility** to understand that it is that same system of government that allows you to demonstrate in the first place, and to realize how rare and precious that right is.

A man has the **right** to look at an attractive woman.

* * * * * *

*H*e has the **responsibility** to keep in mind that she may be someone's wife, daughter and/or mother, and to treat her with the same respect that he would wish his wife, daughter or mother to be treated.

You have the **right** to criticize others.

★ ★ ★ ★ ★ ★

You have the **responsibility** to recognize your own failings and how you feel when others criticize you.

You have the **right** to say that you were unfairly treated.

★ ★ ★ ★ ★ ★

You have the **responsibility** to yourself and your family to do what you need to do about the situation, learn from it, then move on.

You have the **right** to drink.

★ ★ ★ ★ ★ ★

You have the **responsibility** not to drink and drive.

You have the **right** to worship according to your own beliefs.

★ ★ ★ ★ ★ ★

You have the **responsibility** to realize that not everyone shares your beliefs.

Door-to-door and telephone salesmen have the **right** to solicit your business.

★ ★ ★ ★ ★ ★

They have the **responsibility** to recognize that you have a right to your privacy, and that you may not want any of what they are selling.

*Y*ou have the **right** to say that some men physically abuse their wives and girl-friends and that it is always wrong.

* * * * * *

*Y*ou have the **responsibility** to realize that, even according to the most damning statistics, the overwhelming majority of men do *not* beat their wives.

As a juror, you have the **right** to exonerate or convict a defendant regardless of race, creed, color or political correctness.

★ ★ ★ ★ ★ ★

You have the **responsibility** to make your decision based on the facts presented to you.

As a defense attorney you have the **right** to defend a murderer even though you are convinced of your client's guilt.

★ ★ ★ ★ ★ ★

As a member of your community and the human race, you have the **responsibility** *not* to purposely confuse or knowingly mislead a jury or court in order to free a guilty man.

*A*s a prosecuting attorney, you have the **right** to prosecute a defendant to the fullest extent of the law and your ability.

★ ★ ★ ★ ★ ★

*Y*ou have the **responsibility** never to prosecute someone, regardless of the implications politically or personally, whom you believe, or come to believe, to be innocent.

As a juror, you have the **right** to acquit a defendant on the grounds that the prosecution did not prove its case beyond a reasonable doubt.

★ ★ ★ ★ ★ ★

You have the **responsibility** to understand the difference between reasonable doubt and certainty.

*A*s a juror you have the **right** to acquit a murderer because of what you believe to be a greater "just" cause.

* * * * * *

*Y*ou have the **responsibility** to realize that you send the message to others that they can free other murderers on the basis of what *they* consider to be a greater and *more* just cause; you must also recognize that *their* just cause might be in direct opposition to *your* just cause.

*A*s an activist you have the **right** to incite a crowd to action.

★ ★ ★ ★ ★ ★

*Y*ou have the **responsibility** to step forward and claim responsibility for the actions you incited, regardless of whether or not those actions are the ones you anticipated.

$\mathcal{F}$ree speech activists have the **right** to say that everyone has the right to be heard.

★ ★ ★ ★ ★ ★

$\mathcal{T}$hey have the **responsibility** to defend free speech with the same advocacy when someone is saying something they don't like.

Conservative *and* liberal activists have the **right** to peacefully protest against those they believe to be wrong.

★ ★ ★ ★ ★ ★

They have the **responsibility** to allow dissenting voices to be heard, lest their own voice, credibility and right to speak disappear.

You have the **right** to study philosophy and be stimulated by new and exciting ideas.

★ ★ ★ ★ ★ ★

If you plan to live by those ideas or proselytize others to this philosophy, you have the **responsibility** to test the ideas in the laboratory of real life.

Sports fans have the **right** to yell and scream their approval or disapproval at a ballgame.

★ ★ ★ ★ ★ ★

They have the **responsibility** to know when their behavior crosses the line into rudeness and hooliganism.

$\mathscr{Y}$ou have the **right** to own a pet.

★ ★ ★ ★ ★ ★

$\mathscr{Y}$ou have the **responsibility** to remember that you are completely responsible for that pet.

*Y*ou have the **right** to call yourself an American.

★ ★ ★ ★ ★ ★

*Y*ou have the **responsibility** to keep America strong and defend her against those who would seek to destroy the freedoms you enjoy.

You have the **right** to burn the flag.

★ ★ ★ ★ ★ ★

You have the **responsibility** to respect the strength and integrity of a country that gives you the freedom to do so.

*Y*ou have the **right** to be offended.

★ ★ ★ ★ ★ ★

*Y*ou have the **responsibility** to recognize that tolerance is not acceptance, and that if you wish others to tolerate your brilliant ideas and insight, you must tolerate, though not necessarily accept, others whose ideas are not nearly as brilliant and insightful as yours.

You have the **right** to watch boxing.

★ ★ ★ ★ ★ ★

You have the **responsibility** to admit that its purpose is to render one of the participants unconscious or beaten so badly that he cannot continue.

You have the **right** to criticize war veterans.

★ ★ ★ ★ ★ ★

You have the **responsibility** to realize that they gave more for your freedom than you will ever give for theirs.

*Y*ou have the **right** to say that patriotism sucks.

★ ★ ★ ★ ★ ★

*Y*ou have the **responsibility** to recognize that hundreds of patriots died so that you might have the freedom to say that.

You have the **right** to get angry.

★ ★ ★ ★ ★ ★

You have the **responsibility** to get over it.

You have the **right** to watch sports or play golf on religious holidays.

★ ★ ★ ★ ★ ★

You have the **responsibility** to see that your children at least know enough to make an informed decision as to whether or not they want to watch sports or observe the holiday in a religious manner when they grow up.

You have the **right** to gossip.

★ ★ ★ ★ ★ ★

You have the **responsibility** to recognize that when you gossip you say
more about yourself than you say about
anyone else.

*Y*ou have the **right** to counsel your children not to abuse alcohol or drugs.

★ ★ ★ ★ ★ ★

*Y*ou have the **responsibility** to lead by example.

You have the **right** to expect that, with some effort, you can control your reactions to people and things.

★ ★ ★ ★ ★ ★

You have the **responsibility** to realize that you have little, if any, control over what others think or do.

You have the **right** to tell others about your successes.

★ ★ ★ ★ ★ ★

You have the **responsibility** to understand why they are not as interested in your successes as you are.

*Y*ou have the **right** to announce to the world that you are good.

★ ★ ★ ★ ★ ★

*Y*ou have the **responsibility** to be sure you have the "goods" to back it up.

*Y*ou have the **right** to say there are at least two sides to every dispute.

★ ★ ★ ★ ★ ★

*Y*ou have the **responsibility** to understand that every side may not be equally valid.

$\mathcal{TV}$ producers have the **right** to say
that a steady diet of murder, rape, violent
sex and obscene language has no effect
on children or other people who watch it.

★ ★ ★ ★ ★ ★

$\mathcal{T}$hey have the **responsibility** to try
and keep a straight face while doing so.

Movie producers have the **right** to say that Hollywood doesn't create reality, it merely reflects it.

★ ★ ★ ★ ★ ★

They have the **responsibility** to question why Hollywood overwhelmingly chooses to reflect the most negative and aberrant aspects of society.

*Y*ou have the **right** to justify art on the basis that it *is* real life.

* * * * * *

*Y*ou have the **responsibility** to explain why, using that criterion, Rembrandt is now on the same artistic plane as some-one who urinates on a piece of cardboard and puts a frame around it.

*Y*ou have the **right** to say something glib or laugh it off when you hear that a basketball player makes 100 times the salary of a man working on a cure for cancer.

★ ★ ★ ★ ★ ★

*Y*ou have the **responsibility** to come up with a reasonable explanation when your child asks you why this is so.

*Y*ou have the **right** to turn down a menial job because it doesn't pay what you think you're worth.

★ ★ ★ ★ ★ ★

*Y*ou have the **responsibility** to realize that taking welfare and food stamps *instead of* the menial job also says something about your worth.

You have the **right** to go first class.

★ ★ ★ ★ ★ ★

You have the **responsibility** to pick up the tab.

*Y*ou have the **right** to start your own business.

★ ★ ★ ★ ★ ★

*I*n order to make it a success, you have the **responsibility** to possess the knowledge, passion and commitment to hard work that will be required to make it work.

You have the **right** to remodel your home.

★ ★ ★ ★ ★ ★

You have the **responsibility** to make sure your neighbors will not be inconvenienced and to alert them before any work is begun.

*Y*ou have the **right** to have an abortion even though others may peacefully and lawfully protest your decision to do so.

★ ★ ★ ★ ★ ★

*Y*ou have the **responsibility** to realize that others will sincerely disagree with your decision, and to respect their right to *peacefully* express their opinion.

$\mathcal{A}$ homosexual or lesbian has the **right** not to accept the beliefs of those who don't accept him or her.

★ ★ ★ ★ ★ ★

$\mathcal{T}$ hat person also has the **responsibility** to realize that others have the right to not accept his or her beliefs.

You have the **right** to expect tolerance of your religion and sexual preference.

★ ★ ★ ★ ★ ★

You have the **responsibility** not to expect, or need, the acceptance of others.

$\mathcal{A}$ president has the **right** to blame others for the country's problems.

★ ★ ★ ★ ★ ★

$\mathcal{H}$e or she has the **responsibility** to recall that it was another president who once said, "The buck stops here."

The media apparently has the **right** to print or broadcast incorrect or misleading information that can ruin a person's reputation (sometimes because of "deadline pressures").

★ ★ ★ ★ ★ ★

The media has the **responsibility** to realize that this kind of "journalism" has contributed to—though is by no means completely responsible for—people's lack of candor or willingness to stand up and take personal responsibility.

A responsible journalist has the **right** to print the truth.

* * * * * *

A responsible journalist has the **responsibility** to determine what the truth is before it is printed (even if they miss a deadline).

You have the **right** to believe that
money can buy happiness.

★ ★ ★ ★ ★ ★

You have the **responsibility** to understand that while money can always buy
pleasure, it cannot buy happiness.
(Although it can often serve as a pretty
good down payment.)

*Y*ou have the **right** to say that you will make no judgments for, or about, your children.

★ ★ ★ ★ ★ ★

*Y*ou have the **responsibility** for parenting your children and realizing you are their primary role model.

*Y*ou have the **right** to call people out-of-touch and old fogeys for being offended by words in movies, songs or overheard in public.

★ ★ ★ ★ ★ ★

*Y*ou have the **responsibility** to live by your own principles when those people use words you find offensive. (Principles are meaningless when you apply them only to others.)

You have the **right** to be politically incorrect.

★ ★ ★ ★ ★ ★

You have the **responsibility** to not be purposely rude or offensive.

$\mathscr{Y}$ou have the **right** to say that poverty causes crime.

★ ★ ★ ★ ★ ★

$\mathscr{W}$hile poverty may be a contributing factor to crime, you have the **responsibility** to explain why the overwhelming majority of poverty-level people are law-abiding citizens, why rich people commit crimes and why there is much more widespread and vicious crime today than there was during the Depression.

*Y*ou have the **right** to say that an illegal immigrant who gives birth to a baby in the United States is entitled to health care services and welfare.

★ ★ ★ ★ ★ ★

*Y*ou have the **responsibility** to see that the new mother is educated about her responsibilities for receiving those services.

*Y*ou have the **right** to complain that insurance companies don't cover everyone in every situation.

★ ★ ★ ★ ★ ★

*Y*ou have the **responsibility** to realize that, unless we have a Socialist form of government, insurance companies are under no obligation to do so.

$\mathcal{Y}$ou have the **right** to believe that your child is the brightest and the best.

★ ★ ★ ★ ★ ★

$\mathcal{Y}$ou have the **responsibility** to understand that other parents feel the same way about their children (regardless of how misguided they might be).

*Y*ou have the **right** to try out for the team.

★ ★ ★ ★ ★ ★

*Y*ou have the **responsibility** to realize that the decision as to who makes the team is usually someone else's...and not always fair.

STEPHEN SMOKE has dealt with the issue of personal responsibility in many of his seventeen novels, including *Black Butterfly*, *Pacific Coast Highway*, *Tears of Angels* and *Pacific Blues*. He has also written and directed feature films, including *Street Crimes*, starring Dennis Farina. He is the president and CEO of BuddhaScape Corporation, a company that provides Internet and Multimedia products and solutions for business. Mr. Smoke lives in Los Angeles with his wife, Margaret, and Ace, their black Shar Pei.

If you wish to contact Mr. Smoke, or if you wish to connect with other people in order to discuss some of the issues raised by this book, *The Bill of Responsibilities* Internet site can be reached through the following Internet address:

http://www.buddhascape.com

★ ★ ★ ★ ★